# 50
## fantastic things to do with
# Pre-schoolers

## SALLY AND PHILL FEATHERSTONE

Featherstone

# Contents

Published 2010 by A&C Black Publishers Limited
36 Soho Square, London, W1D 3QY
www.acblack.com

ISBN 978-1-4081-2330-0

Written by Sally Featherstone and Phill Featherstone
Design by Sally Boothroyd
Photographs © Shutterstock 2010

This book is produced using paper that is made from wood grown inmanaged, sustainable forests. It is natural, renewable and recyclable. The logging and manufacturing processes conform to the environmental regulations of the country of origin.

To see our full range of titles
Visit www.acblack.com/featherstone

# Introduction

There's plenty of research to show that babies and children who enjoy a stimulating home environment learn better and more quickly. So what parents and carers do to lay the groundwork for learning early on is an investment that pays back throughout their child's life.

This book has been specially written for parents to use with their young children at home. However, it can also be used by carers and workers in nurseries and childcare settings. It contains 50 simple activities that can be done easily with very little equipment, often in odd moments of time. It's not a course to work through. All the ideas here are suitable for children from 36-50 months, and in many cases beyond.

Choose what you and your child enjoy as one of the main aims of this book is fun! There are few things as delightful or rewarding as being alongside young children as they explore, enquire, experiment and learn. Join them in their enthusiasm for learning!

There are four books in the 50 Fantastic Things series:

**50 Fantastic Things to Do With Babies** (suitable for use from soon after birth to 20 months)

**50 Fantastic Things to Do With Toddlers** (suitable for use from 16–36 months)

**50 Fantastic Things to Do With Pre-schoolers** (suitable for use from 36–50 months)

**50 Fantastic Things to Do With Four and Five Year Olds** (suitable for use from 40–60+ months)

The age groupings above are approximate and are only suggestions. Children develop at different speeds. They also grow in spurts, with some periods of rapid development alternating with other times when they don't seem to change as quickly. So don't worry if your baby doesn't seem ready for a particular activity. Try another instead and return to it later. On the other hand, if your baby gets on well and quickly, try some of the ideas in the 'Another idea' and 'Ready for more?' sections.

# A NOTE ON SAFETY

Care must be taken at all times when dealing with young children. Common sense will be your main guide, but here are a few ideas to help you have fun safely.

Although rare, swallowing objects or choking on them are hazards. Some children are more susceptible than others.

Young children's lungs are delicate. They need clean air. *Never* smoke near your child, and don't allow anyone else to do so.

Children are naturally inquisitive and you will want to encourage this. However, secure and happy children are often unaware of danger. Your child needs you to watch out for them. Make sure you are always there. You can't watch your child all the time, but don't leave him/her alone and unsupervised for more than a few minutes at a time. Even when they are asleep check on them regularly.

The objects and toys we suggest here have been chosen for their safety. Nevertheless, most things can be dangerous if they go wrong or are not used properly. Please take care.

What is your child learning?

*Your child is learning that routines are predictable and important. This activity will help them feel secure and comfortable.*

# Bedtime teddy!
## practising routines

*What you need:*

- *a teddy or doll with removable clothes*
- *a 'babygrow' or pyjamas for the teddy (desirable, but not essential)*
- *baby toothbrush*
- *flannel*
- *a doll's bed or a box for a bed*
- *some fabric for bedclothes – an old pillow case and a fleece would be good as they don't fray*

**Ready for more?**

Make this game a regular feature of bedtime, so your child begins to have a sense of responsibility for their toy.

WHAT TO DO:

1. Make the bed ready for the toy. Let your child put the pillow and sheets on and cover them with the fleece.

2. Now ask your child to tell you what the toy needs to do before they go to bed. Help them to think by talking about what they do before they go to bed.

3. Find some of the things your child talks about, a toothbrush and toothpaste, a flannel, a comb, a story book, a tiny teddy for the toy. Now help with getting the toy ready for bed, talking with your child as they prepare the toy.

4. When the toy is safely tucked in bed, you could read a story and give them a cuddle.

5. Now help your child to be a parent by clearing up and putting away all the things you used, tiptoeing around so as not to wake the teddy or doll. Then you could have a cuddle too!

**Another idea:** If the teddy or doll is waterproof, you could give them a bath before you put them to bed. Or you could give them a pretend bath in an empty washing-up bowl.

HELPFUL HINTS

Some children find it difficult to remember things in abstract. They might find it easier to play this game in the bedroom or bathroom.

# Mine and yours
## naming and recognising objects

*What you need:*
*Some pairs of objects – one of yours, one belonging to your child, such as:*

- *your hat and their hat*
- *your shoe and their shoe*
- *your hairbrush and theirs*
- *your sock and their sock*

**WHAT TO DO:**

1. Sit with your child, and look at all the things you have collected.

2. Now take a pair of objects.

3. Hold both objects out to your child and, using their name, ask (for example), 'Which is Evan's hat? Which hat is yours?'

4. Encourage them to look carefully and choose the object that is their own.

5. Praise their efforts and say 'Yes, that's your hat. This is my hat.' Play again.

**Another idea:** Encourage your child to sort the objects and clothing into two piles.

**DID YOU KNOW?**
It takes many children a while to recognise themselves as a separate person.

**Ready for more?**
Add some baby or doll's clothes to the game and sort three ways, asking 'Who does this belong to?' Let your child fetch the doll or teddy to join the game.

**HELPFUL HINTS**
If your child finds it difficult to recognise their own belongings, remind them each time they get dressed by saying 'This is your coat isn't it Matt? We are putting on Matt's coat.'

Put a coat hook low down in your hall, so your child can begin to find, and look after their own belongings.

## What is your child learning?

*This game will help your child to know they are a separate person and that they have belongings. This is a great step in learning to be independent.*

# Stamp and clap
## wrist bells

**What you need:**
- *some baby wrist toys – bells and rattles*

**WHAT TO DO:**

1. If you haven't got any wrist toys, find some bracele or bangles for your child to wear. Several of these will make a good sound.

2. Keep the wrist toys out of sight till you have practised this little song. You could sing it to th tune of Frère Jacques:

   *I am clapping, I am clapping
   Here I come, here I come
   Can you see me clapping, can you hear me clapping
   Here I come, here I come.*

3. You can change the words to add 'stamping' 'shaking' or 'waving' for more verses.

4. Now bring the wrist toys where your child can see them, and offer them some to wear on their wrists or ankles. You could wear some too.

5. Sing the song again and clap your hands as you sing.

   **Another idea:** Collect a basket of gloves and play the same game with these.

**DID YOU KNOW?**
Clapping along to music is good for body control.

**HELPFUL HINTS**
If your child finds it difficult to listen and move at the same time, play the game sitting on the settee or the floor.

**What is your child learning?**

*Your child is learning how to coordinate their hands and feet. This will help them to strengthen the muscles in these areas of their body.*

What is your child learning?

*Feeling the different textures and talking about what they are and how they feel will help language development. Discussing the properties of what's in the trays increases knowledge and understanding of the world.*

# Bare feet
## textures and feet

*What you need:*

- *four plastic trays, washing up bowls or box lids (they don't all have to be the same size or shape)*
- *warm, soapy water and a towel*
- *cold, wet sand*
- *tiny pebbles or gravel*
- *fur fabric or a small blanket*

**Ready for more?**

Try making footprints on black paper with water.

Put some paint on a tray or tin lid and draw with your feet.

**WHAT TO DO:**

1. Put some warm, soapy water in one tray or bowl. In the second put a layer of cold, damp sand. Put some pebbles in the third. Cover the base of the fourth with the fur fabric or blanket.

2. Take off yours and your child's shoes and socks. Play a game of 'copy me', wiggling toes, pointing them in the air, walking on heels, etc.

DID YOU **KNOW?**
*Feeling different textures stimulates the sensory receptors in the brain.*

3. Feel the coldness of the kitchen floor, the texture of the living room carpet, etc.

4. Take turns to step into and out of each tray. Start with the sand and finish with the water. Don't rush it, and talk about what you are doing and how it feels.

5. Work your way through the trays and finish with a dip in clean, warm water, tickling toes as you dry them.

**Another idea:** Walk on other textures – sandpaper, clay or mud, feathers – and talk about how they feel.

# Fingers and thumbs
## finger painting

### What you need:

- *big sheets of paper*
- *aprons*
- *a washable surface*
- *some finger paints – you can make these at home*
- *a bowl of warm water and a towel*

### WHAT TO DO:

1. Put your aprons on.

2. If you want to make your own finger paint, help your child to mix a few tablespoons of cornflour or flour with some water. Add some food colouring. Put each colour in a separate saucer.

3. Put the paper on a flat surface on a table or the floor.

4. Put the saucers or pots of paint in the middle of the table and show your child how to scoop some of the paint onto the paper. Move the paint around with your fingers and the palms of your hands. Use both hands and show that you are enjoying it!

5. Now let your child explore the paint with their fingers and hands.

6. Don't worry if your child makes a mess, painting is messy!

7. As soon as they have had enough, let them wash their hands in warm bubbly water.

**Another idea:** Finger painting doesn't need paper. You can use any flat surface such as a work surface in your kitchen or the inside of the bath.

### Ready for more?

Give your child a toy car to run through the paint, making tracks through the paint and onto the paper.

Make hand prints by putting your hands in the saucers and printing them on paper or card. Talk about the differences between your hands and theirs.

## HELPFUL HINTS

Some children don't like getting their hands messy. This sort of play is very important, as it helps your child to exercise their fingers and hands. Encourage them and show them you like the activity.

Make sure you don't get anxious about the paint getting all over your home. Do this in the kitchen, or out of doors, where you will both feel more relaxed.

**What is your child learning?**

*Your child is learning about the texture of things and how they behave when they push and poke them.*

## HELPFUL HINTS

If your child finds the dough play difficult, help them to flatten the dough and show them how to pat it with a flat hand.

Some children find it hard to separate their first finger. Don't worry, they soon will! Pointing activities help, or gently help them to curl the other fingers round out of the way. Don't force it.

What is your child learning?

*Your child is learning that cooking, stirring and mixing activities with you are fun. They will also be learning about how things change in cooking and mixing.*

# Pat a cake
## making pastry

### DID YOU KNOW?
*Wrist, hand and finger muscles are all important for drawing and writing. Start young!*

### *What you need:*
- *flour*
- *water in a mall bottle or jug*
- *a bowl*
- *a spoon*
- *a board, table or worktop space*
- *aprons*

### WHAT TO DO:

1. Put on your aprons.

2. Help your child to spoon six tablespoons of flour into the bowl and pour a little water on it.

3. Your child can mix the flour and water to make a thick dough, adding more water if it's too thick, more flour if it's too sticky.

4. When the dough sticks together, help your child to lift it out onto the board or surface.

5. Now make some dough for yourself.

6. Pat and poke the dough together with fingers and hands.

7. Sing the 'Pat a Cake' song:
   *Pat a cake, pat a cake, baker's man*
   *Bake me a cake as fast as you can*
   *Prick it and toss it and mark it with 'B'*
   *And put it in the oven for Baby and me.*

8. Change the letter and name to the name of your child.

**Another idea:** You could bake the pastry, but it doesn't taste very nice!

### Ready for more?

Add some margarine or butter to the pastry mixture and stick some raisins in the cake. Bake this one and you *can* eat it.

Use bought pastry for 'Pat a Cake' game or to make some jam tarts. Even young children love doing simple cooking and offering it to the family.

# Colour spray
## using hand sprays

**DID YOU KNOW?**
*Some children don't achieve 20/20 vision until they are about two years old.*

### What you need:

- *some spray bottles (get ones that are easy to squeeze and check that the trigger isn't too far away for small hands to grip)*
- *thin paint or food colouring mixed with water (red, blue and green should be enough)*
- *paper or fabric*

### WHAT TO DO:

*You need a fine day for this activity.*
*The aim is to make a picture using a spray and colours.*

1. Pin or tape a sheet of paper or fabric to a fence or outside door.

2. Fill the spray bottles with the colours (thin paint or food colouring plus water).

3. Encourage your child to experiment with the sprays. You may need to show them how to work the spray first, but don't take over the painting!

4. You might want to distract your child with something else while the first lot of paint dries, and then carry on later.

5. When your child's masterpiece is dry don't throw it away but use it. You can pin it up in his/her bedroom, use it for wrapping paper, paste it to the lid of their toy box

   **Another idea:** Use a spray with clean water to wash outdoor toys.

### Ready for more?

Paint a simple picture on a smooth surface and encourage your child to use a water spray to wash it off.

Use a spray to water plants or wash windows.

### HELPFUL HINTS

Be prepared to give your child help if s/he finds it hard to use the spray bottle. You may get wet, but it's good fun!

Try holding a piece of absorbent paper, such as a paper towel, in front of the spray to get a good effect.

### What is your child learning?

*To begin with your child may simply spray in all directions! However, let them have several goes over a number of days and they will probably start to think about what they are doing and compose the colours.*

# Through the tunnel
## enjoying play tunnels and tents

*What you need:*

- *a play tunnel or pop-up play tent (if you don't have one you can make one by draping a sheet or blanket over a couple of dining chairs or a clothes airer)*

**Ready for more?**

Make up a simple story about a monster, your child and the tunnel or cave. Role-play the story.

WHAT TO DO:

1. Involve your child in the preparations. Let them watch and help you put up or make the tent or tunnel. If you are making it yourself use plenty of tape and/or pegs to fix the sheet securely to the chairs or airer.

2. Sit at one end of the tunnel. Encourage your child to crawl through it to you. It's helpful if you can do this with another adult, so your child can crawl between you. If not, getting them to crawl towards a favourite soft toy should get them started.

3. Praise your child when s/he gets to the end of the tunnel.

4. Be a fun monster and chase your child into the tunnel. Don't get serious – keep it light hearted.

**Another idea:** Reverse the roles – have your child chase you!

DID YOU **KNOW?**
Most children love dens and enjoy looking out at the world from somewhere safe.

HELPFUL HINTS

Some children are anxious when starting this activity but most really love it once they get into it. If your child is anxious, start with a very short tunnel (little more than a hoop). Or try making the tunnel out of a net curtain so they can see out.

Hang some bells on ribbons from the roof of the tunnel, so your child crawls through them.

What is your child learning?

*This activity is good for physical development and for encouraging exploration and spatial awareness. Developing the story will stimulate creativity.*

**DID YOU KNOW?**
*Finger play is important for developing brain connections.*

# Stickers and stars
## fun with fingers

*What you need:*
- some washable felt-tipped pens
- some small, self-adhesive labels
- a selection of star stickers (different colours if possible)

**Ready for more?**

Make a collection of rings, bracelets and necklaces (or make some yourself out of coloured wool). Play at putting these on each other and on soft toys.

**WHAT TO DO:**

1. Put a star sticker on both of your child's index fingers and on your own.

2. Hold your index fingers in the air. Wave the stars about. Start with the stars high up, reaching as high as you can, and swoosh them down like shooting stars.

3. Hold your stars up again and sing, *Twinkle, Twinkle Little Star*. Encourage your child to join in. Shake your fingers to make the stars 'twinkle'.

4. Now put a star sticker on every one of your child's fingers, and on all yours. Sing *Twinkle, Twinkle Little Star* again.

**Another idea:** Draw bird shapes on stickers and stick them on your hands. Sing the *Two Little Dicky Birds* rhyme and do the actions.

What is your child learning?

*This activity helps development in a lot of areas – fine movement and control, language, linking words with actions, copying and imitating.*

# Transparent colours
## a colour-changing treasure basket

**What you need:**
- a basket full of multi-coloured objects (e.g. transparent coloured paper and shapes, coloured fabrics and netting, kaleidoscopes or viewers
- a white blanket, sheet or rug.

**WHAT TO DO:**

1. Spread out the sheet, rug or blanket on the floor. Place the basket of transparent coloured objects on it.

2. Together explore the contents of the basket. Pick them up one by one and look at them. Take turns to peer through the kaleidoscopes and viewers. Talk about them – their colours, how they make things look, how they feel.

3. Try layering one of the transparent objects over another. How does this alter the colours? Move one over the other and look at how the colours change.

4. Ask your child simple questions and encourage her/him to repeat some of the words you are using to describe the objects and how you are playing with them.

**Another idea:** Add lots of coloured objects to bath time play.

**DID YOU KNOW?**

Bright colours stimulate the brain and encourage lively activity.

**Ready for more?**

Shine a torch through coloured plastic or cellophane, on to a white sheet. Use several colours to make a pattern.

Play with coloured water in plastic bottles (food colouring or a dash of paint in water works well).

What is your child learning?

*This activity is about exploring and investigating. It not only contributes to understanding colours and objects but also stimulates creativity.*

### HELPFUL HINTS

See if you can have in your basket some objects that are both a mix of colours and an interesting texture (e.g. plastic bangles, hair scrunchies).

What is your
child learning?

*Your child is
learning that
their choices
are important
to you, and
that choice is
part of every
day.*

DID YOU **KNOW?**

*Some children are natural 'snackers' and may need a very small meal every hour!*

# Veggies and dips
## snack time choices

### *What you need:*

- *vegetables to cut into 'dippers' – carrots, celery, peppers, cucumber*
- *little breadsticks*
- *plain yogurt*
- *tomato ketchup*
- *chopped chives*

**Ready for more?**

Help your child to put toppings such as cream cheese on small snack biscuits, and top these with tiny pieces of tomato, green pepper or cucumber.

Offer small pieces of fruit and chopped raw vegetables in an ice cube tray to tempt them to choose.

### WHAT TO DO:

*This activity is about making healthy choices.*

1. Let your child watch or help as you divide the yogurt into some little bowls, leave one plain and make some flavoured dips with the rest.

2. Now cut the vegetables into sticks and arrange these on a plate. Use vegetables that your child likes, with perhaps one new one. Put out some breadsticks or a few crisps too.

3. Now sit with your child for a snack. Remember that your child will be influenced by your behaviour and your choices, so make good choices yourself! Talk about what you choose and encourage your child to try things.

4. The important thing is to get your child to try things, so if they try something and don't like it, don't force them to eat it.

**Another idea:** Have choices of vegetables with meals whenever you can. Let your child help themselves – they will have a good idea of how much they can eat. Be sure to praise them for trying new things.

# My baby
## baby doll play

### What you need:
- a baby doll
- baby clothes, nappies, bottle, comforter
- a cot, blankets, pram or stroller

*This activity isn't only for girls. It's important for males to develop caring and nurturing skills too. Besides, most boys will enjoy playing with dolls at this age.*

### WHAT TO DO:

*This activity isn't just for girls. It's important for males to develop caring and nurturing skills too. Besides most boys will enjoy playing with dolls at this age.*

1. Sit down with your child, the baby doll and the various items you've gathered. Talk about them and what they are all for.

2. Talk to the doll, and talk to your child about the doll. Give him/her a name. Take turns to cuddle and stroke the baby. (If you have two dolls it sometimes works better to have one each, but still talk and play together.)

3. Start to role-play being a parent. The baby is sleepy. Rock him/her gently and sing a nursery rhyme. When the baby is asleep (let your child decide when this is) lay them down and cover them up.

4. Talk about your baby being tired, hungry, or needing to be changed. Go through the play of meeting these needs – feeding, changing, putting to bed. At each stage talk about how the baby feels. Encourage your child to contribute words and ideas.

**Another idea:** Young children are usually fascinated by babies. If there's a baby among your friends or family try to let your child spend some time with them.

### Ready for more?

Play with toy baby animals and toy people. Talk about how animals and people look after babies and keep them safe.

Look at mother and baby books and books about baby animals. Look out for DVDs and television programmes to watch. Talk together about the book or DVD.

## HELPFUL HINTS

Some baby dolls are quite large. Make sure you have one which is small enough for your child to handle comfortably.

Learn some new baby songs. There are lots of internet sites that have them, some with tunes as well as lyrics. Put 'lullaby songs' in Google. (NB. If you put 'baby songs' in your search engine you'll get pop songs instead of children's songs!

What is your child learning?

*Learning to care, and demonstrating caring and loving, are important as your child moves beyond an exclusive focus on self and towards becoming aware of the needs and feelings of others.*

# Just like me
## an action game

**What is your child learning?**

*Imitating and copying are among the main techniques your child has for learning. Watching you closely and following what you do will also develop their observational skills.*

**What you need:**
- *a selection of soft toys*

**WHAT TO DO:**

1. Start by sitting down with your child. Tell them that you want them to do everything you do.

2. Wave your arms in the air and sing, '*Wave your arms, wave your arms, just like me.*' Encourage your child to copy you. Reward them with praise and smiles when they do.

3. When your child has got the hang of this sing, '*Shake your head, shake your head, just like me*' and encourage copying. Go on with waggle your hands, rub your chest, pat your knees, and so on.

4. Take a soft toy each. Move the toy and sing, getting your child to shadow the toy's movements and join in, e.g. '*Look at teddy jumping, look at teddy jumping, way up high.*'

**Another idea:** Repeat an action you've done before but with a minor change. Encourage your child to watch closely and copy you exactly.

### Ready for more?

Let your child take the lead, choosing actions or deciding what to put on or take off. Follow them, and encourage them to talk about what they are doing.

Play a 'follow me' game around the house, going into and out of rooms, walking in silly ways, making gestures.

### DID YOU KNOW?

*Movement along with words is a strong reinforcer of links in the brain.*

### HELPFUL HINTS

If your child needs help starting, begin with toys that make a noise. Have one each, you make the noise and they copy.

Lots of repetition will help your child get the most out of this activity, so don't move on from one stage to another too soon.

What is your child learning?

*Tidying up for your child will not teach them and will irritate you. Learning that objects have clear places to go is an important organisational skill. This activity, with plenty of fun and rewards, will help your child learn the importance of organising and looking after their own possessions.*

# Everything in its place
## clearing up

**What you need:**
- a basket of items belonging to your child, collected from around your home

**WHAT TO DO:**

Use this game to help your child learn the proper places for things, and have fun putting them away!

**DID YOU KNOW?**
Research suggests that our primitive ancestors (800,000 years ago) demonstrated tidy behaviour.

1. Tip the objects out of the basket on to the floor.

2. Pick one up. See if your child can name it. Ask if they can tell you where it belongs. Be prepared to give them clues if they don't know.

3. Once you've established where the item goes, ask your child to take it there. You may need to go with them to help with doors, drawers and lids. Once they've put the item away successfully give lots of praise. Then ask your child to choose another item.

**Ready for more?**

It may take your child some time to get the hang of this and be able to tell you where things go. Help them to think and work it out, but if they can't do this, help by taking them to the place and showing them.

Have a 'clearing away basket'. Encourage your child to use it to put their toys away.

**Another idea:** Play a reverse version of the game. Give your child the name of an object and ask them to find it and bring it to the basket.

# Snip snap
## early cutting

### What you need:

- child's scissors (i.e. 'safe' scissors with rounded ends)
- plenty of scrap paper (junk mail, old magazines, wrapping paper, envelopes)

### WHAT TO DO:

*This activity is about self-assurance and confidence in the use of a tool for cutting. It's not about accurate cutting out.*

1. Cut some of the paper into long thin strips. Your child needs to be able to snip across the strips in one cut.

2. Leave some of the paper in larger pieces.

3. Sit down with your child. Show them how to hold and use the scissors. Be sensitive to hand preference by getting them to try both hands and settling on the one they find most natural. Talk about cutting and snipping.

4. Encourage your child to cut the papers, snipping the long strips into bits and snipping round the edges of the larger pieces.

5. Give help if it's needed by holding the paper as they snip, or by putting your hand over theirs on the scissors.

**Another idea:** Work together to make some place mats by snipping the edges of squares of coloured paper in a fringe.

**Ready for more?**

Fringe the edges of a drawing or painting.

Make a pattern by cutting coloured and shiny paper into strips and sticking them on card.

For a change, let your child hold the paper while you snip.

## HELPFUL HINTS

You can get special scissors for left handers, but many toddlers are still experimenting with both hands, so satisfy yourself that your child really is left handed before buying these.

## What is your child learning?

*Using scissors is a good example of simple tool operation. It requires higher levels of co-ordination of hand, eye and movement. Lots of practice will develop facility in handling not only scissors but other tools too.*

# Rocking teddy
## a rocking snuggle song

**What you need:**

- a blanket or piece of soft fabric – stretchy fabric works best
- a cushion
- a favourite soft toy or teddy

**WHAT TO DO:**

1. Put the cushion on the floor and sit your child on it.

2. Sit down opposite. Give your child the soft toy and wrap the blanket gently round their shoulders.

3. Grip the blanket firmly at the edges and rock gently from side to side.

4. As you rock gently with your child opposite you, rocking in the blanket, sing:

*Rocking softly, rocking slow*
*Gently gently, here we go.*
*Hugging Teddy, keeping warm*
*Keeping safe and out of harm.*

The tune to *Twinkle Twinkle Little Star* works well, or you can make up your own.

**Another idea:** Sing and play *Row Row Row the Boat*. You can find the words and tune by searching in Google.

**DID YOU KNOW?**

Anxiety or stress release chemicals in the brain which inhibit learning.

**Ready for more?**

Use a blanket to make a small hammock for soft toys. Rock them gently, singing this song or *Rock a Bye Baby*. When you have played the game, hang the hammock above your child's bed, cot or changing mat.

### HELPFUL HINTS

This is a good activity to do with very active children and works well after a bath and before bed. It will help your child feel safe, secure and probably sleepy.

What is your child learning?

*Feeling safe, secure and valued helps the development of self-confidence and self-assurance. It also encourages feelings of trust.*

What is your child learning?

*This activity will help with concentration and perseverance. Your child will also be learning the crucial actions of bringing their finger and thumb together in a 'pincer movement'.*

# Five little peas
## popping and placing

**What you need:**
- *some peas in their shells*
- *small bowls*

**Ready for more?**

Say this rhyme. You need to make a fist and open your fingers one at a time as the pod pops:

*'Five fat peas in a peapod pressed, one grew, two grew, so did all the rest.'*

*'They grew and grew and did not stop, till one fine day when the pod went 'POP'!'*

**WHAT TO DO:**

1. If the peapods are muddy, give them a quick wash.

2. Sit in the kitchen with your child, and look at the peapods, and any leaves or tendrils that are attached to them. Talk about the peapods growing on a plant in a farmer's field.

**DID YOU KNOW?** Using both hands stimulates both sides of the brain.

3. Show your child how to press their thumb on the end of the pod (not the stalk end) so it pops open. Listen for the little 'pop'.

4. Now show them how to carefully open the pod so they can see the peas all in a row. Count them together. Let them take the peas out of the pod and put them in a bowl.

5. Look at the inside of the peapod and how it is shaped to fit the peas.

**Another idea:** Scrub some potatoes together and sing *'One potato, two potato'* as you put your fists one on top of the other.

# Let's eat
## making a simple snack

### *What you need:*
- *bread*
- *a toaster or grill*
- *butter or substitute*
- *blunt knives (little butter knives or plastic picnic knives are ideal)*
- *something to spread on top – jam, honey, cheese spread, etc.*

### WHAT TO DO:

1. Get all the above items together. Make sure the butter is taken out of the fridge in good time, so it's not too hard.

2. Tell your child you're going to make a snack.

3. Make some toast. Stress the importance of keeping away from hot things, but let your child be involved by watching you.

4. Cut the toast into half or quarter slices.

5. Talk to them about the spreads you have available and choose one for them to spread. Encourage them to ask you for what they want, using 'please' and 'thank you' as you pass things to each other and waiting for answers.

6. Give your child help spreading if they need it, but the more s/he can do for her/himself the better.

**Another idea:** Go shopping with your child for the ingredients for their snack.

### What is your child learning?

*Independent activities which involve negotiation and choice encourage brain growth. Making a choice also develops the concept of action and consequence.*

### Ready for more?

Plan a picnic. Involve your child in choosing, getting together and packing the food.

Let your child make their own lunch or after-care snack. Try making something more ambitious than toast – beans on toast, or even a simple pizza.

### HELPFUL HINTS

Too many choices can bewilder some children. Limit what's on offer to start with.

Give attention to using the correct words for things, and to using the knife properly for spreading.

# Making faces
## a book of expressions

*What you need:*

- *a collection of magazine pages with people's faces showing a range of expressions (newspaper colour supplements and celebrity magazines are good sources)*

**Ready for more?**

Play 'How Do I Feel'. Make a face and ask your child to say what you are feeling. This makes a fun family game.

**WHAT TO DO:**

This activity is quite sophisticated and therefore suitable for children who are older. If your child doesn't seem to get it, put it aside and try again in a few weeks.

1. Sit in a comfortable chair with your child and look at one of the magazines. When you come to a picture of a face ask your child how they think that person is feeling.

2. Find a photo of someone smiling. Look carefully at their mouth and eyes. Ask your child if they can make a smiling face. Praise them when they get it right.

3. Now say, 'Can you make your face sad (or grumpy, or cross, or disappointed? Keep looking at the pictures and practise different expressions together.

4. Talk about how you feel when you're happy, or cross, or sorry, or sad.

5. Talk about how you know what other people are feeling. 'How do you know when Mummy's cross?' Or 'How do you know when (friend's name)'s upset?'

HELPFUL HINTS

For an easier start, pick out a few extreme expressions – e.g. somebody laughing or crying – and talk about those first.

Use a mirror so you child can see his/her expressions and practise them.

**Another idea:** When you read stories to your child talk about how the people in the story are feeling.

## What is your child learning?

*This game will Learning to 'read' and empathise with another person's feelings is a key human skill. This activity will help your child to begin to think about and respond to how other people feel.*

# Fetch it for me
## under a blanket

**What you need:**
- a big sheet of fabric, such as an old sheet or curtain
- a basket of objects to hide – soft toys, cars, a ball

**WHAT TO DO:**

1. Spread the sheet on the carpet or the grass.

2. Sit at the edge with your child, lift the sheet and peep underneath.

3. Lift the edge right up and put it over your heads so you can see right under the sheet. Can you see to the other side?

4. Now take a soft toy, fold the sheet back, put the toy down and pull the sheet over it. For the first time, put the toy quite near the edge to build confidence.

5. Ask your child 'Can you see where Teddy is? Can you go under the sheet and fetch him?' if your child is hesitant go under together and fetch the toy.

6. Play again with a different toy. Praise them for being 'brave'.

**Another idea:** Let your child go under the sheet and hide a toy for you to fetch. Help them by holding the edge of the sheet to help them.

**Ready for more?**

Play 'Chase the Feet'. Take off your shoes and put your legs under the sheet. Move them around and let your child see if they can catch them through the sheet.

### HELPFUL HINTS

Use a small blanket to play 'Guess What?'. Put some toys under the blanket and see if your child can guess what they are by feeling through the blanket or by just putting their hands under.

Some children are really frightened by this sort of game. Stay with them, and make sure the sheet is small enough for them to stand up and get out when they want to.

What is your child learning?

*This game will build your child's confidence. They are learning that you are a constant feature of your life and that you will keep them safe.*

# My bath crayons
## more mark making

**DID YOU KNOW?**
*Activities like this will stimulate the whole brain!*

**What you need:**

- a pack of bath crayons
- a flat plastic lid for each of you (from plastic boxes)
- nail brushes, old toothbrushes and sponges
- warm soapy water and a towel
- aprons or old clothes

**WHAT TO DO:**

1. Put a bit of water on the lids to make them damp.

2. Now experiment with the bath crayons, making marks, circles, wiggly lines. Talk about what you are doing – this will keep your child focused.

3. Keep showing each other what you have done, and give praise for effort and different sorts of marks.

4. When you have plenty of bath crayon on your lids, have a go with nail brushes, old toothbrushes or sponges to move the colour round the lid and make patterns in the colours.

5. When you have finished help your child to wash the lids and their hands in warm soapy water and dry them carefully.

    **Another idea:** Take long bits of string outside and trail them through puddles or bowls of water and then along the path or patio.

**Ready for more?**

Let your child help with washing up by offering a washing up brush to clean cutlery and plastic plates etc.

What is your child learning?

*Your child is learning that they can make their own marks with no fear of being 'right' or 'wrong'. This is very important in building a 'can-do' attitude.*

**HELPFUL HINTS**
Stick the lid to a table or the floor to stop it sliding around as your child works.

# Can you find?
## animal sounds

*What is your child learning?*

*Talking and playing games lets your child know that you are interested in them. This is an important thing for children to learn. Confident children who feel secure and valued make better progess.*

**What you need:**

- *some 'small world' toy farm animals – familiar ones such as a cow, pig, sheep, chicken, horse, cat, dog*

**WHAT TO DO:**

**1.** Start the game by playing with the animals and making their noises. 'Walk' them across the carpet towards each other making the sounds.

**2.** Now say, 'I'm going to ask you a question. Are you ready?'

**3.** When your child is ready, say 'Can you find the animal that says "Moo"?'. When your child fetches the animal, reward them with praise and smiles.

**4.** Continue to play with the different animals, making the sounds for your child as clues.

**5.** If they want to ask you a question, let them.

**6.** When your child has had enough, play a different game with the animals, or leave them for free play.

**Another idea:** Sing '*I Went to Visit a Farm One Day*' as you play with the animals. Find the words and the tune on the Internet.

### Ready for more?

Make a scrapbook of animals, cutting the pictures from magazines or using clip art from the Internet.

If your child has a favourite animal, make them a photo book of cats, dogs, elephants, whatever they choose.

### DID YOU KNOW?

*The more words your child hears, the faster they will learn language.*

### HELPFUL HINTS

Every time you play a new game, go slowly to start with. Watch your child, just play for a short time, and play the same game again after a few days so they get used to it.

Just use two or three animals when you start the game, and reduce distractions by switching off the TV or radio.

**DID YOU KNOW?**

Mark making in messy play helps children's brains get used to recognising patterns.

# Fingers and thumbs
## mark making in shaving foam

**What you need:**
- some shaving foam in an aerosol (un-perfumed and non-allergenic)
- pieces of card, scissors
- old loyalty or credit cards, sticks and sponges
- a flat, washable surface, such as a worktop

**WHAT TO DO:**

1. Sit with your child and talk about shaving foam and look at the can together.

2. Now spray some foam on the flat surface and let your child explore it with their hands and fingers.

3. Join in and play with them, using your fingers to make marks in the foam. Encourage your child to make circles, swirls, zigzags or even letters, but keep it free and fun.

4. Cut some pieces of card about 8 cm long. Cut zigzags and other shapes in the edge of each piece to make patterned scrapers.

5. Now try making marks with the scrapers you have made or use old credit or loyalty cards.

**Another idea:** Add some paint or food colouring to the foam.

**What is your child learning?**

*Your child is learning skills that will prepare their hands and finger as well as their brains for the important tasks of reading and writing.*

**Ready for more?**

Try finger paint or foam on the tiles by the bath for some 'easy to wash off' fun together at bath time.

# Snap, crackle, pop
## making sounds with feet and hands

**What you need:**
*A range of fabrics and materials that make sounds:*
- *bubble wrap*
- *tissue paper*
- *chocolate box or other food liners*
- *foil*
- *empty crisp packets*

**WHAT TO DO:**

1. Put all the materials you have collected on the floor.

2. Sit with your child and look at all the things. Experiment with scrunching, popping and feeling with your fingers.

3. Now take off your shoes and socks and stand up to explore the materials with your feet. Stamp, hop and jump on the fabrics, popping the bubble wrap, scrunching the tissue, flattening the chocolate box liners and crisp packets.

4. Talk about how they feel – 'crinkly, poppy, crunchy, smooth' and how they sound 'like fireworks, like raindrops.'

**Another idea:** Collect some smooth, fluffy and soft materials and objects for a different sort of feeling.

### DID YOU KNOW?
Playing with bare feet improves balance and movement, as it strengthens foot muscles.

### Ready for more?

Try painting on bubble wrap or foil, using paint with a little white glue added.

Take your shoes and socks off and walk round your house, feeling all the different surfaces and textures with your feet and toes.

What is your child learning?

*In exploring textures and objects with hands and feet, your child is finding out about the world.*

### HELPFUL HINTS

Hold your child's hands if they are still a bit wobbly on uneven surfaces. This activity is very good for balance and confidence.

Some children don't like being barefoot. Make sure the room is warm and comfortable and just have bare feet for a short time.

## HELPFUL HINTS

Don't worry if your child holds the pens and crayons in their fist. They will learn later how to hold them like you do. Just keep on giving a good model for them to copy.

Make sure you are clear about where children can draw and where it is not allowed. Clear rules are more important than taking materials away when they use them inappropriately.

**What is your child learning?**

*Learning about tools such as pens and other mark makers is the first stage in learning to draw, write, dig, eat, hammer etc. This activity gives your child practice and an adult model to follow.*

# A basket of markers
## exploring colours

**DID YOU KNOW?**
*Children get a great sense of security from clear rules, but don't have too many!*

### What you need:
- a big piece of paper and masking tape, which peels off without damaging surfaces
- some children's big felt pens or crayons
- a flat vertical space – the back of a door, the front of a big fridge, a big piece of card from a packing box

**Ready for more?**

Find a place in your house where you can display your child's mark making and first 'pictures'.

### WHAT TO DO:

1. Stick the paper on the flat surface, make it reach right down to the floor and up to the highest point your child can reach. Put the basket of crayons or markers on the floor by the paper.

2. Sit or kneel with your child in front of the paper and encourage them to start making marks. Remember that mark making is a first stage and comes before drawing objects or people.

3. Join in and talk together about what you are doing. Use simple colour words as you work, and describe the marks – 'I'm doing some wiggly lines up here at the top' 'I'm going to use the red now'.

4. Continue to draw until your child has had enough or, leave the drawing so they can come back and add more marks later.

**Another idea:** Use bath crayons at bath time or on a worktop in the kitchen.

What is your
child learning?

*Completing this
activity over time
helps your child to
learn the importance
and reward of a
longer term project.*

## HELPFUL HINTS

Short sessions of this activity over time will help to build
concentration. Don't try to finish the collage in one session.

When your child is busy doing something else (or sleeping)
prepare some things to add to the collage by cutting out
a few small pictures or finding something that supports a
current interest, such as animals, tractors, trains. Put these
in a bowl near the collage and add a glue stick.

# Get the big picture
## make a really big picture

**What you need:**

- newspaper, wallpaper or a roll of drawing paper
- a big piece of card
- masking tape or sticky tape, scissors (round ended), glue sticks
- stickers, magazines, junk mail, old greeting cards, gift wrap etc

**Ready for more?**

Add glitter, sequins, gift ribbon, scraps of fabric and lace, family photos, clip art, even tiny toys – a collage can contain anything!

**WHAT TO DO:**

*This is a longer activity, so be prepared to have it around for several days or even weeks!*

1. Cover the big piece of cardboard entirely with paper, wrapping the paper over the edges and sticking it securely on the back with tape.

2. Find a place to put the card – prop it against a wall, stick it to a door, put it on a table.

3. Now collect all the things you need to make a picture collage – see **What you need**.

4. Talk about the 'Big Picture' and what your child would like to do. Remember, the collage won't be a traditional picture of one thing, but a collection of smaller pictures, patterns and textures covering the whole sheet.

5. Cut or tear out any pictures that catch your eye and stick them on. If you put the card on the floor or a table, your child can work from any side.

6. When your child has had enough, prop the picture up and have a look. Then put the picture somewhere safe, but where your child can see it and continue to add new pictures and objects over time.

**Another idea:** Make a family photo collage with photos of family, friends, favourite toys, holidays and special occasions.

**DID YOU KNOW?**

Looking, talking, choosing and adding pictures reinforce naming objects.

## What is your child learning?

*Children learn just as well from simple games that use everyday objects. This game helps them to track a moving object in space and use their hands and eyes in a coordinated way.*

# Falling feathers
## clap and catch

### What you need:

- feathers (get these from a craft shop or online)
- chiffon scarves (charity shops are good places to find these)

### WHAT TO DO:

*If you find feathers on walks, make sure they are clean by washing them thoroughly in hot soapy water and drying them before use.*

1. Sit with your child and tell them you are going to play a catching game.

2. Put the basket of objects nearby, but not where it will distract your child.

3. Take a small chiffon scarf from the basket and hold it high above the child's hands. Say 'Ready, steady, GO!' then drop the scarf for your child to catch.

4. Do this several times so they get used to the catching.

5. Now take a small feather from the basket, and gently stroke your child's hands or cheek.

6. Hold the feather up high above your child's hands and say 'Ready, steady, GO!' before dropping the feather for your child to catch. This is harder than catching the scarf, so use smaller, curly feathers which will fall more slowly than bigger ones.

7. Keep dropping feathers and scarves for them to catch, reminding them to watch the object as it falls.

**Another idea:** Blow some bubbles for your child to catch with both hands. Blow them up above them, so they have time to watch and catch.

### Ready for more?

Make some small balls from rolled socks and use these for catching and throwing, or throw them into a waste paper basket or bucket.

When you are washing hands or in the bath, drop wet flannels and sponges for them to catch.

# Wet and dry
## sand play

### *What you need:*
- *some play sand*
- *a washing up bowl or a big plant saucer*
- *small sieves, funnels, plastic bottles, corks, yogurt pots, spoons*
- *a water jug*

### WHAT TO DO:

1. Sit with your child and let them watch as you pour dry sand into one of the trays or bowls.

2. Play with them, using the sand toys and containers. Look at the sand, and how it pours and moves.

3. Now take out the toys, put some water in a plastic jug and let your child add this to the dry sand a bit at a time. Watch what happens.

4. Try not to interfere with your child's exploration of the wet sand. They may want to put lots of water in, or just a tiny bit.

5. When the sand is damp offer your child some containers or sand moulds to make castles and shapes.

**Another idea:** Add some toy animals or cars to the damp sand tray. Help your child to make mountains, fields or a zoo.

### Ready for more?

Offer your child water play in a bowl in the sink. Give them some warm bubbly water and add some plastic spoons, small pots and pans, yogurt pots etc.

### What is your child learning?

*Feeling different textures and changing things by adding water are ways that all children learn about the world.*

### HELPFUL HINTS

Most children love sand and water play. If your child does not, just play with dry sand to start with and offer small amounts in a little plastic bowl.

For some young children the aim seems to be to get as much sand as possible out of the container and onto the floor! Make sweeping up part of the game.

What is your child learning?

*Making toys from simple objects is a useful lesson for children and families. Successful learning often comes from using familiar objects in a new way.*

# Bouncing balls
## fun with elastic

**DID YOU KNOW?**
*Watching a bouncing object will strengthen your child's eye muscles.*

### What you need:
- *elastic bands*
- *some long pieces of thin elastic, about 35 cm (18 inches)*
- *newspaper, old wrapping paper or paper towels*

### WHAT TO DO:

1. Help your child to scrunch a piece of newspaper or old wrapping paper into a ball about as big as your fist. Press it hard to make it as solid as possible.

2. Fix the ball together with elastic bands, so it is a good shape and firm enough to bounce. Try it by bouncing it on the floor.

3. Now tie a piece of elastic round the ball to make a bouncing toy.

4. Play bouncing games with the ball, up and down the stairs, round the room, in the garden, on a walk to the park.

5. Make a new ball when your old one wears out.

**Another idea:** Make a waterproof ball by putting the paper ball in a plastic bag before fixing it with elastic bands. Now you can play in the rain or even in the bath!

### Ready for more?

Tie elastic onto soft toys and take them for a bouncy walk. Be attentive when your child is out of doors, they will be concentrating on the ball and may not be as aware of other things.

# Up and down stairs
## climbing and looking

**What you need:**

- *the stairs in your home, or some safe steps in a park*

### Ready for more?

Sing the same song as you go up an escalator. This is sometimes easier for your child as they don't have to concentrate on stepping and looking at the same time.

Take a teddy up the stairs, counting as you climb, and saying 'One step Teddy, two steps Teddy, Three steps Teddy'. Go up to five, then start counting again.

**WHAT TO DO:**

1. Stand at the bottom of the stairs with your child, holding their hand.

2. Start to climb the stairs one at a time, at your child's pace.

3. As you climb the stairs, say or sing '*Up the stairs and up the stairs and up the stairs we go. Up we go and up we go and up we go again.*'

4. Keep singing as you climb to the top.

5. Now look at what you can see from the top of the stairs. 'What can we see from the top of the stairs? I can see your bed!' or 'I can see the shops.' If you are in the park, find a place to sit and watch the people going by. If you are at home, sit on the top step, looking down to see what you can see.

6. Go down the stairs, saying or singing '*Down the stairs and down the stairs and down the stairs we go. Down we go and down we go and down we go again.*'

7. If your child wants to up again, do it. If not, sit on the bottom step and see what you can see.

### HELPFUL HINTS

If your child is still learning about stairs, stand behind them and put your hands under their arms to help them.

Find steps and low walls in your favourite places, such as the park, and practise simple songs and counting as you walk.

**Another idea:** Practise counting as you climb the stairs. Don't worry if your child can't count accurately yet. Listening to you counting will help them a lot.

## What is your child learning?

*Watch your child to see how they climb. An early stage is to lift one foot up (or down) a step, then bring the other foot up (or down) to join it. This is quite normal, and some children walk downstairs in this way for a long time.*

### DID YOU KNOW?

*Stepping or climbing stairs is a great way to get into the rhythm of counting.*

# The hat dance
## a stopping and starting game

**What you need:**

- a collection of hats – helmets, sunhats, caps, bobble hats (make sure at least one of the hats fits you)
- a full length mirror so the children can see themselves
- some music on an MP3 player or CD player

**WHAT TO DO:**

1. Spread all the hats out on the floor and walk between them with your child, looking at the different hats.

2. Turn on the music and walk or dance round the hats. When the music stops, choose a hat each, put it on and dance around the hats.

3. When the music stops, take off the hat and put it back on the floor.

4. Play again and choose a different hat and do a different dance.

5. Go on as long as your child is enjoying the game.

6. When you have finished, toss all the hats back into a basket or box.

**DID YOU KNOW?** Stopping needs lots of practice. Your child's brain needs more time to stop than an adult's does.

**Another idea:** Put a pair of gloves by each hat. When the music stops, you must put on the hat *and* the gloves.

**Ready for more?**

Play the hat game again and this time take another hat every time the music stops. How many hats can you balance on your head?

Play some more stopping and starting games. How many blocks can you put in a bucket before the music stops? or How many pens can you put in a cup?

## What is your child learning?

*Moving confidently is a skill every child should learn. Give your child lots of opportunities to move rhythmically to music.*

### HELPFUL HINTS

Some children get so involved in dancing that they don't hear the music stop. Make sure you wait until they have really stopped.

Get some plastic plates and wooden spoons, or some pots and metal spoons, and have a marching band. Using your whole body helps with a sense of rhythm.

# Spongy feet
## squidgy feelings

*What you need:*
- *a flat space outside and a warm day*
- *a big piece of foam sheet (a camping mattress is ideal)*
- *silver 'Duct' tape (from Bargain shops or DIY stores)*
- *baby bubble bath mixed with a little water*
- *a towel*

WHAT TO DO:

1. Put the foam sheet on a smooth floor outside, and tape it down securely. Now pour some bubble bath and water mixture on the sheet. Not too much!

2. Take your shoes and socks off, and roll up your trousers. Help your child to do the same. Put the towel nearby but not too close.

3. Now hold hands with your child and step onto the foam. Start to move around. Your feet will make bubbles come out of the foam.

4. Keep walking and stamping so you make a real bubbly mat of foam on the foam!

5. When you have had enough, step carefully off the edge of the foam mat and dry your feet on the towel.

**Ready for more?**

Fix sponges on your feet by pulling socks over them. Step in bubbly water, then on a dry path or patio to make bubbly footprints.

**Another idea:** Try the same game with a big sheet of bubble wrap, securely taped down.

What is your child learning?

*Balance is an essential skill for all physical activity. This is a good way to practise. Your child is also learning to try new experiences, which will link more cells in their brain.*

HELPFUL HINTS

If your child is less steady on their feet, hold both their hands. This will give them more confidence.

This activity makes some children very excited. Use a low, calm voice and keep the activity short. Help them to calm down afterwards by wrapping them in a big warm towel and singing a quiet song.

## HELPFUL HINTS

Some children are frightened of putting their hand in a bag if they can't see inside. Let them feel the bag outside first, so they feel more confident.

If they are not sure of the object use, gently take their hand and help them to brush their hair or yours, to feed a doll or teddy etc.

What is your child learning?

*Your child is learning to link objects with their uses. This is an important part of organising their world.*

**DID YOU KNOW?**
Using the sense of touch makes learning links in the brain stronger and more permanent.

# I wonder?
## collections in a feely bag

*What you need:*
- *a fabric bag such as a shoe bag, or a pillowcase*
- *some items round a theme, such as:*
- *bathroom things – a comb, toothbrush, toothpaste, flannel*

*or*
- *food*

*or*
- *clothes*

### Ready for more?

Play the feely game with toys. Start with just one toy in the bag. See if they can name it and ask them for a colour if they are beginning to know these.

**WHAT TO DO:**

1. Start the activity with the objects on the floor next to the bag.

2. Sit with your child and look at all the objects, naming them and talking about how they are used.

3. Now put the objects in the bag and let your child feel in the bag and see if they can name the object before they pull it out. Say 'Can you feel it? What is it? Now 1-2-3 let's look!'

4. Have a go yourself and see what you can find. Exaggerate the '1-2-3 let's look!' so your child is anticipating and listening to you.

5. See if your child can guess the hidden object if you say 'I can feel something that you use to clean your teeth. Can you guess what I can feel?'

6. Continue playing until your child has had enough. Then let them help you put the things away.

**Another idea:** Just put one object in the bag and see if they can guess what it is by putting their hand in the bag or feeling from the outside.

**What is your child learning?**

*Your child is learning that taking turns can be fun. This will reinforce the pleasure your child takes in playing with others.*

# My turn, your turn
## a turn taking game

**What you need:**
- *stacking bricks in a basket or box*

**WHAT TO DO:**

1. Sit on the floor with your child. You will need a flat surface for brick building, so avoid carpets or rugs.

2. Take one brick out of the basket and put it on the floor.

3. Say 'Your turn', and encourage your child to put a brick on top of yours.

4. Now continue to take turns building the bricks till the tower falls down. Make this enjoyable by saying, 'Here it goes – crash, bang, all fall down'.

5. Now ask 'Again?' and build the tower again together. Most children will play this game again and again.

6. When you or they are tired, take turns to toss the bricks back in the basket one at a time.

**Another idea:** Build towers with cans or cartons from your kitchen cupboard. These may make wobbly towers, which are even more fun.

**Ready for more?**

Start the tower, then ask each other for a particular brick. 'Now can you put a red brick on?' 'Which colour shall I put next?'

Play 'Thank you' with the bricks – 'Can you give me a blue brick?' 'Thank you, now can you give me a red brick?' Use a soft toy to help – 'Can you give Teddy a brown brick? Thank you.'

HELPFUL HINTS

Clearing up is part of playing a game. Make it fun by having a gentle race or asking for a particular toy or brick.

Some children find it difficult to take turns and wait for another person to have a go. Praise their efforts when they do wait.

# Who am I?
## simple dressing up with a mirror

**What you need:**

- a safe mirror at child height
- plastic sunglasses, or empty glasses frames
- simple dressing up items – scarves, hats, jewellery, shoes, handbags
- face paints if you have them

**WHAT TO DO:**

1. If there is a long mirror in your hall, your own bedroom or your child's room, you could play the game there.

2. Put the dressing up things on the floor and sit or kneel by your child, so you can both see both of you.

3. Now try on some of the dressing up clothes together, talking about how you look in them. Ask your child's opinion – 'Do you like this hat, or this one?' 'Do you think I look like Daddy in these glasses?'

4. Encourage your child to pretend to be other people as they try on the clothes.

5. Sing a song or do some funny walking as you look at yourselves in the mirror.

6. If you have similar objects, follow your child and dress up just like them. This will cause a lot of amusement.

**Another idea:** Make some face paints from moisturiser with food colouring added, put it in little pots for your child to use, and make a little 'dressing table' from a box or small table, adding combs, brushes and hand mirrors.

**Ready for more?**

Add some cloaks and masks for superhero play, or some fairy tale clothes to play storytelling. Children love grown up clothes such as high-heeled shoes, ties and jackets.

Take some photos of yourselves in the mirror, and print them or send them to friends and relatives.

### HELPFUL HINTS

Some children find buttons and other fastenings difficult. Dressing up is a great way to practise.

Looking at their own face in a mirror helps children to recognise their own features and learn how others see them. They will begin to understand themselves as a separate being.

DID YOU
**KNOW?**
Getting dressed and
undressed uses both
hands and both sides
of the brain.

What is your child learning?

*Pretending to be someone else teaches
your child about feelings and the way
other people act. This helps them to
develop social skills and empathy.*

DID YOU
**KNOW?**
*Following and copying will improve your child's attention span focus.*

What is your
child learning?

*Your child will be
learning how to
copy movements
and instructions.
This is great
preparation for
later life, when
they will need to
concentrate and
follow others.*

# Touch your nose
## learning body parts

**What you need:**

- *no special equipment needed for this activity*

**WHAT TO DO:**

1. Sit opposite your child on the floor or the settee.

2. Tell them you are going to play a game called 'Put Your Finger on Your Nose'. Explain that you will tell them what to do and they must copy you.

3. Now put your finger on your own nose, saying 'Put your finger on your nose'. Ask your child to copy you and praise them when they do.

4. Continue to play the game, saying the instruction and doing it your self – use movements and words like 'Put your finger on your hair, your knee, your foot etc' or 'Put your hand on your head, your leg, your back etc'.

5. If they want to continue, try with two hands – 'Put your two hands on your cheeks, your feet, your neck etc'.

6. Sing the song 'Put Your Finger in the Air'. Find the words with a Google search.

**Another idea:** Play the game with a doll or soft toy each. 'Put your finger on Teddy's tummy, on Teddy's ear etc'.

### Ready for more?

Play the same game standing up.

As your child gets used to this game, give them instructions *without* doing the action yourself. See if they can follow your words, but don't go too fast and give them clues of they are finding it difficult.

Make the game even more complicated by asking them to do two different things – 'Put one hand on your head and one hand on your tummy' or 'Put your finger on your tummy and your foot in the air'.

### HELPFUL HINTS

Sit closer if they are having difficulty copying you, or help them by holding their hand.

Match the game with the body parts your child knows – eyebrows and eyelashes, ankles and thighs may be too difficult at first.

**What is your child learning?**

*Your child is learning that mealtimes are special occasions, and that the conventions of meals, such as politeness, passing things etc. are important and valuable skills to learn. They will also learn hand control from serving, pouring and cutting food.*

# After you!
## taking turns and sharing

### What you need:

- a child's teaset or some plastic picnic plates, cups, jug, cutlery etc
- some pretend or real food
- Milk, juice or water
- A small table and a cushion each

### WHAT TO DO:

1. Help your child to set out the table for your tea party, talking about how many plates, cups etc you need.

2. Sit on a cushion each and begin to play tea parties. Concentrate on sharing and being polite.

3. Pour drinks and pass round the food together, remembering to ask what the other person would like, and talk about what you are doing.

4. Model good behaviour by saying 'Please' 'Thank you' 'Could you pass?' 'Would you like..?'

6. When your child copies you, praise their behaviour, by saying 'That was really polite' or 'You shared those really well'.

**Another idea:** Sometimes let your child lead your meal and serve you for a change!

**DID YOU KNOW?**
Eating meals together as a family helps children to develop language and social skills.

**Ready for more?**

Have picnics on the grass or even indoors on wet days, but concentrate on good manners and polite behaviour. Model the behaviour you want your child to learn.

# Sticker fun
## following instructions

*What you need:*

- *some sheets of stickers or stars (get these from stationery shops or toys shops)*
- *camera or phone with a camera*

**WHAT TO DO:**

1. Look at the stickers together and talk about them if they have pictures on.

2. Now explain that you are going to ask them to put the stickers in funny places on their body!

3. Hand them the first sticker and say 'Can you put this sticker in your leg?'

4. When they have done that, continue the game by asking them to put stickers on other parts of their body or clothes.

5. Praise them each time they get it right.

6. When they have had enough, or you run out of stickers, take a photo of your child before the stickers start to drop off!

**Another idea:** Put the stickers on a teddy or a favourite toy.

### DID YOU KNOW?

Knowing and naming parts of the body is a vital skill in your child's development.

### Ready for more?

Make the game more complicated by asking your child to stick the stickers on their face while they are looking in a mirror – this is difficult, even for adults!

Use a picture in a magazine of an animal or a person. Play the game again, putting stickers on the picture.

What is your child learning?

*Apart from learning about their own body, this game provides lots of practice in following instructions. Watch your child carefully and expand the list by using more difficult names of parts of their face and body.*

### HELPFUL HINTS

If your child has not had much practice in using stickers, let them experiment before giving precise instructions. Go slowly, and make the game simple.

**DID YOU KNOW?**

Blowing bubbles helps children's breathing, and this helps with talking.

# Bubble and blow
## fun with bubbles

*What you need:*
- *some bubbles and blowers*
- *straws*
- *scissors*
- *small plastic bowls*
- *an old towel for drips and spills*

**WHAT TO DO:**

*This is a good activity to do in the garden or the park.*

1. Play with the bubble pots and blowers, holding the blower for your child if they find it difficult.

2. Watch the bubbles as they float, and talk about the colours, shapes and sizes. Catch them and pop them.

3. Blow some bubbles near your child so they can reach or chase them.

4. Now cut a small nick about 2 cm (1 inch) from the top of a straw. Some children get mixed up between blowing and sucking, and this will stop them swallowing the bubble mixture!

5. Put some bubble mixture in a small bowl and show your child how to blow gently into this mixture to produce a pile of bubbles.

**Another idea:** Mix some bubble mixture with food colouring and make some bubble prints by blowing into a bowl of bubbles and putting a sheet of paper over the top to make a print.

What is your child learning?

*Getting involved in simple activities like blowing bubbles, helps in the early stages in realising that children can do things for themselves. This will help their confidence.*

**Ready for more?**

Find a small battery powered fan. Use this to blow the bubbles around indoors and outside.

Use coat hangers or bendy twigs to make giant bubbles in a washing up bowl of bubbly water.

# Noodle heads
## playing with textures

### What is your child learning?

*Using hands and fingers with tactile materials teaches children to manage slippery stuff. It also helps them to concentrate by offering them interesting and unusual materials to work with.*

### *What you need:*
- *a pack of instant noodles*
- *a big plastic bowl*
- *cooking oil*
- *small plastic plates*
- *glitter, sequins*

### WHAT TO DO:

1. Cook the noodles by pouring boiling water over them in a bowl, then drain them thoroughly and let them cool.

2. Now help your child to mix the noodles with half a teaspoon of cooking oil to stop them sticking together.

3. Work together to spoon the noodles onto some plates and sit with your child to play with them.

4. Practise picking up just one noodle between your finger and thumb. Take the noodle to an empty plate and gently put it down. Use spoons and forks to lift and share the noodles. Sprinkle sequins or glitter on top to make dinner for each other.

5. Have a noodle party with some soft toys.

6. When you have finished playing put the noodles in the garden for the birds to eat.

**Another idea:** Try the same game with cooked spaghetti. Colour the spaghetti by putting food colouring in the cooking water.

### Ready for more?

Cut the big sides from cereal packets and save these for painting and tactile experiences like this. Make patterns on these cards and the starch in the noodles will stick them without glue.

Picking up small objects such as dried peas or small buttons and putting these in a tin will challenge your child's concentration and dexterity.

### DID YOU KNOW?
*Careful movements with finger and thumb are essential for writing.*

### HELPFUL HINTS
Using tweezers is another way of keeping children involved as they learn to manage fingers and hands. Get some plastic ones suitable for children.

## HELPFUL HINTS

Some children find it difficult to isolate their first finger. You may need to gently help them curl their other fingers back.

Pointing and poking fingers in holes is an action that fascinates many children. Be patient as they investigate every hole as you go for walks or shopping.

What is your child learning?

*By exercising hand and finger control in enjoyable activities your child is learning essential skills for learning to write, draw and use all sorts of tools.*

# Poking, poking
## finger play with dough

**DID YOU KNOW?**

*Pointing is a good thing to practise. It is a first step in holding tools such as pencils.*

### What you need:

- a rolling pin
- a flat surface for rolling out the dough
- to make some simple dough you need:
- 4 cups of flour
- 2 cups of table salt
- 2 cups of warm water
- a wooden spoon
- a bowl

### WHAT TO DO:

1. Help your child to measure and mix the dough. Put the salt and flour in the bowl and mix thoroughly.

2. Now add the warm water a bit at a time, mixing between each addition.

3. When the mixture makes a soft dough, tip it out of the bowl and let your child play with it without any intervention from you.

4. Help them to roll out some of the dough into a flat cake and play a poking game, using your first finger on each hand to make finger pokes all over the dough.

5. Gather the dough up again, roll it out and play again, seeing who can make the most 'pokes' in the dough.

6. When you have finished, put the dough in an airtight plastic bag in the fridge, it will keep for several days.

### Ready for more?

Roll some of the dough into sausages and let your child cut these into bits with children's scissors.

## What is your child learning?

*In this game, your child will be learning about shapes and sizes by matching them against their own bodies. Looking at baby clothes helps them to understand about growth.*

# Giant feet!
## getting an idea of size

**What you need:**
- a full length mirror at child height (in the hall or a bedroom)
- very big clothing such as: adult gloves, hats and socks, wellies, big flipflops, men's shoes, slippers
- Very small clothing such as baby shoes and socks, little pyjamas, baby mittens

**WHAT TO DO:**

1. Collect all the clothes and mix them up in a washing basket. Sit with your child near the mirror.

2. Help them to take the clothes out of the basket, talking about them and who they could fit. Try to use two word descriptions such as 'Big boots' 'Little baby socks'.

3. Try some of the clothes and shoes on. Look at yourselves in the mirror.

4. Ask them if they think any of the clothes fit them, or if they would fit you. Put on some of the biggest things yourself and say 'Too big!' Put your feet next to the baby shoes and say 'Too small!'

5. Sort the clothes into a pile of big ones and a pile of small ones. Now put them all back in the basket.

    **Another idea:** Use the collection of clothes to have a family dressing up race. Make it harder for the adults by giving each adult a doll or teddy to dress in the baby clothes as well as dressing themselves. Take some photos.

**Ready for more?**

Take some photos of the clothing and shoes. Make these photos into a Snap or Pairs game where you match the big and small pairs.

**HELPFUL HINTS**

Some children may get distracted, by the baby clothes. They may just want to talk about being a baby. If so, get your baby photos out and look at them together. Leave the game for another day.

**DID YOU KNOW?**

Sorting and recognising different sizes is important for mathematical development.

# Sort it out
## sorting natural objects

**What you need:**
- *baskets or boxes for sorting*
- *a big shallow basket or box*
- *a collection of natural materials such as*
  - *shells*
  - *stones*
  - *cones*
  - *twigs*
  - *leaves*

**WHAT TO DO:**

1. Put a collection of natural objects in a big box or basket.

2. Arrange some smaller containers (baskets, boxes, bowls) near the collection.

3. Now begin to look at the objects you have collected. Remind your child of the place and time when you collected the object. Talk about what it was like, the weather, what you were doing.

4. Now look closely at the object. Talk about the texture, colour and pattern. Feel the surface against your hands or even your cheek. Does it smell of anything?

5. Now look at another of the objects. Try to choose something that looks or feels different.

6. After you have looked at some of the objects, you could begin to sort them into baskets.

**Another idea:** Make sure your child has some toys made from natural materials such as wood, and encourage them to collect natural objects on walks and visits.

**Ready for more?**

Collect or buy some natural objects such as shells, cones, polished stones, plants, driftwood. These will all give a sense of calm to your home.

When you collect objects on walks, include photos of the place where you went, so you can make a photo book to go with your collection of memories.

**HELPFUL HINTS**

Use a small collection, perhaps just four or five objects while your child develops their language skills.

What is your child learning?

*Your child is learning that natural objects have as much interest as shop bought toys.*

# Who is that?
## recognising faces

**What you need:**

- some photos of family members in different places, clothes and seasons

**WHAT TO DO:**

*This simple activity should be a frequent part of your child's life, celebrating and remembering family occasions and people they know.*

*Framed photos of family members and friends make a real contribution to your child's life. Make sure there are plenty of these in your home.*

1. The photos can be printed on paper, in an album, viewed on a computer or on a mobile phone. (Make sure your phone has a big enough screen for the child to see the faces.)

2. Make sure your collection contains some photos of grandparents, family friends, children and your child too!

3. Sit with your child in a comfy chair or on your knee as you look at the photos.

4. Ask them if they can name the person or people in each photo. Remind them of the occasion and place where the photo was taken.

**Ready for more?**

Help your child to tear or cut photos of faces from magazines and make a scrapbook of faces.

**HELPFUL HINTS**

Recognising yourself in photos is difficult for some children. Take your time and play plenty of photo games.

Take photos of your child regularly and show them the photo as soon after taking them as you can. Digital cameras and mobile phones are great for this!

**Another idea:** Make photo books of holidays and special occasions and have these handy to look at when you have a few minutes spare.

## What is your child learning?

*Your child is learning a sense of self and of community, recognising themselves and the key people in their lives. This will help them to feel more secure and safe.*

## HELPFUL HINTS

The big space is daunting for some children,
that's why staying with them is so important,
so you can give them support and confidence.

If your child finds the tools difficult to use, let
them just play with the paint in their hands.

# Dabbers and dots
## early painting

**What you need:**
- children's paint
- dabbers (you can buy these or stick some foam on chopsticks or ice lolly sticks)
- big paintbrushes
- big pieces of paper (newspaper or the back of wallpaper will do)
- sticky or masking tape, aprons

**WHAT TO DO:**

1. Help your child to stick a big piece of paper to a low table, to make a really big painting surface.

2. Put some paint in plastic mugs or small empty water bottles. If you cut the tops off these and put them back upside down, the tops will fit in the bottoms of the bottles to make non-spill paint pots. These bottles also slow down the drying out of paint!

3. Put your aprons on, put the paints where your child can reach them, and offer the paintbrushes and dabbers.

4. Suggest that your child can stand up to paint if they like.

5. Stay with your child as they paint and join in if they invite you (but don't take over, and don't try to make it a picture!).

6. The idea is to explore the paint and applicators, not to paint 'a picture'.

7. When the painting is finished and dry, find a space to pin it up so everyone can see your child's work.

**Another idea:** Leave the painting activity out all day so your child can return to it more than once.

**DID YOU KNOW?**
Using tools is the first step to writing, give your child plenty of practice in using simple tools.

**Ready for more?**

Ask a friend with a young child to come for a painting morning and join your children for a group painting session in your garden.

Use the dabbers and brushes with a bucket of water to paint the path, fence or back door.

What is your child learning?

*Your child is learning to work on a big scale, to use tools and to persevere with a big project. They may need your help and encouragement to stay focused.*

# Up in the air
## tossing Ted in a blanket

**What you need:**
- a teddy or other favourite soft toy
- a piece of fabric about 1 metre square (stretchy, fleece or knitted fabric is best)
- a space to move about in

**WHAT TO DO:**

1. Explain to your child that you are going to play a game with Ted (or another favourite toy). Show them the fabric or blanket, and practise holding a corner in each hand so you can lift and bounce together.

2. Now put the fabric on the floor and put teddy in the middle.

3. Carefully pick up two corners each and gently lift teddy into the air.

4. Begin to bounce teddy so he moves up and down on the blanket. Say, 'Ted is bouncing, bouncing, bouncing, Ted is bouncing in the air.'

5. Now bounce a bit harder so teddy goes further up into the air. Say, 'Higher, higher, up and down, Ted is bouncing up and down'.

6. Now gently lower the blanket and give ted a hug together.

**Another idea:** Let your child lie on the blanket and take the corners. Gently lift them and swing to and fro.

**Ready for more?**

Try the same game with a balloon. This is more difficult to do, as the balloon is lighter and more likely to fall off the edge.

What is your child learning?

*This game is about trust and working together. Your child will be learning how to control their actions so the game works for Teddy.*

## HELPFUL HINTS

Some children need help to hold on with both hands. If your child's grip is weak, don't bounce too hard or they will lose their hold.

Some children get over-excited, so you need to play the game very gently and use a quiet tone of voice.

**What is your child learning?**

*Your child is learning about being safe and exploring the concept of being lost. Talking about these feelings is very important for your child's development.*

# Lost!
## caring for a lost toy

### *What you need:*

- *a soft toy that your child doesn't know*
- *a luggage label or some card and string*
- *scissors*

### Ready for more?

Make up a story about the lost toy, inventing some of the things he/she has done, where they came from and even who they belonged to.

### DID YOU KNOW?

*Imagining and empathising are called 'higher order' thinking skills.*

### WHAT TO DO:

*This game needs you to keep a secret!*

**1.** Write a message on the label. It can say anything you like, but it should go something like this:
*I am lost and cold and hungry. Please look after me.* Tie the message round the neck of the soft toy.

**2.** Hide the toy where your child will find it the following day e.g. sitting on the back step. Let your child find the toy and read the label to them.

**3.** Now talk about being lost and what you should do with the toy. Accept your child's suggestions, they may want to give the toy a name, some food, make a bed for it, put up a notice to find its owner. Try to respond positively to what they say.

**6.** When your child has lost interest in the toy, you have a decision. You could remove the toy and leave a note from their owner who has come to fetch them; or you could say that no-one is coming so the toy should live with you permanently.

# Jelly on the plate
## play with familiar substances

**What you need:**
- some small plastic plates
- a packet of jelly or some jelly crystals
- hot water
- two plastic bowls
- spoons, forks, a whisk

**WHAT TO DO:**

1. Make the jelly in advance and put it somewhere cool to set.

2. Sit at a table or worktop with your child.

3. Spoon some jelly onto a plastic plate for each of you.

4. Explore the jelly with fingers, hands, spoons and forks. Encourage your child to really get involved in feeling the jelly, squeezing it between their fingers and fists, patting it and pushing it round the plate.

5. Now let your child help you to whisk some of the jelly in another bowl. Explore the jelly with your hands and fingers.

**Another idea:** Put some objects in the jelly before it sets – pieces of paper, polystyrene, beads, glass 'nuggets', even small toys and let your child find them.

### DID YOU KNOW?

Playing with these materials is a vital part of strengthening your child's hands.

### Ready for more?

Have some finger fun with custard or yogurt on a small tray, drawing and making marks with fingers and hands.

Freeze some very small items in ice cubes, tip these out in a bowl of water and play with these as they melt and release the objects.

### HELPFUL HINTS

If your child has any skin allergies, let them experience these activities in gloves.

Some children don't like playing with these tactile materials. Warming some custard or yogurt slightly sometimes makes a difference to their feelings. Or try putting them in plastic 'zip-lock' bags. Close the zips and play with the bags from the outside.

### What is your child learning?

*Your child is learning about textures and the behaviour of solids and liquids. This play will be essential for your child's early science.*

# Inside!
## make a den

### What you need:

- a cardboard box, big enough for your child to get inside
- a blanket, some ushions
- a soft toy or two
- a thin scarf or a piece of net curtain, tape
- a CD player with some quiet music

### Ready for more?

Get into the habit of using boxes and cartons. Make one into a house for a teddy or doll, with a bed and table.

Join some boxes together with tape in a line to make a train with carriages. Fill the carriages with toys. Let your child 'drive' the train from the first box.

### WHAT TO DO:

1. Put the box on its side, and invite your child to climb inside the house. If you can get a really big box, you could get in too!

2. If you can't, sit or lie down next to the box house so you can talk to your child.

3. Ask them if they would like some things to make their house. Offer cushions, a blanket, a soft toy or teddy.

4. Suggest that some music would be nice, and get a player if they want one.

5. Ask your child is they would like a door on their house. If they do, then tape a piece of very thin fabric over the door by taping it across the top of the opening.

6. Most children love being inside boxes, so if your child likes their house, suggest they might like a snack and a drink inside. Sit outside the house to have a snack too, and talk to them through the curtain.

**Another idea:** Use empty cartons for boats, buses and trains. They are free, good play value and disposable – the best sort of toy!

What is your child learning?

*Being in his/her own space helps your child to feel secure and in control. They will also be learning about being quiet and reflective. Quiet activities release calming chemicals in the body and brain. These help your child to learn.*

## HELPFUL HINTS

Pretending is difficult for some children. Model being a pretender yourself, and keep the play simple and short.

Use superheroes or television characters to inspire role-play with cartons and boxes. This will often involve boys in making superhero homes, vehicles etc.

# Stretchy, scrunchy
## fun with wrists and ankles

*What you need:*

- *some bracelets or hair 'scrunchies'*
- *lengths of ribbon or strips of interesting fabric*
- *a basket*
- *some music on tape, CD or radio*

**Ready for more?**

Dance outside to your own songs or a portable player or radio.

**WHAT TO DO:**

1. Show the ribbons and scrunchies to your child and help them to put some on their wrists, arms, and ankles.

2. Experiment with different sorts of dancing steps, swirling, twisting, waving, jumping.

3. Now put some music on, something gentle and floaty would be good. Dance with your child, holding their hands, following their steps, dancing together and by yourself.

4. Ask your child if they would like to do a dance for you to watch. If they do, be appreciative of their effort and give them praise.

5. Try a dance all round the house together.

**Another idea:** Find or buy some bells, add these to the bangles and scrunchies for dances.

**DID YOU KNOW?**

*Music and dancing will help your child to learn. Rhythm helps memory.*

## HELPFUL HINTS

Dancing is a talent that some children have and some don't. Encourage all your child's efforts, however uncoordinated they might be. They will get better with practice!

Some boys (and girls) think dancing is 'girly'. Remind them of the strong male dancing they see on TV and films. Make sure you play more powerful music sometimes, and offer a good range of colours to wear.

What is your child learning?

*A sense of rhythm and a love for dance and music are both good things for children to learn, and the younger they learn them the better!*